FAMILY
SECRETS

BY

MARY ANN OLSON

ISBN-13: 978-0-9891247-3-7
ISBN-13: 978-0-9891247-4-4

PREFACE

All families have secrets. Some are embarrassing, hidden or ignored. Others are meant for the telling. The family secrets shared here are the most precious of all times. All faiths have access to these seeds of wisdom. We are all members of one family searching for the one true God.

The fact that human beings all over the planet Earth intuitively worship something is proof that God has written this in our hearts. It's part of our spiritual genetics.

Cary Schmidt
Newington, Connecticut

The Bible has the answers to all secrets our struggling humanity requires for spiritual growth.

How can faith be real? You can't see it or touch it. One has to take a leap of faith. Everything worthwhile is a leap of faith. Faith matters as it inspires us to raise our sights to live an immeasurably better life. Hebrew 11:1: "Faith is the substance of things hoped for, the evidence of things not seen."

Let us all take the first step in faith;
you don't have to see the whole
staircase, just take the first step.

Dr. Martin Luther King, Jr.

TO THE MEMBERS OF
All FAMILY TREES
A WISH FOR LOVE, HOPE & FAITH

LOVE

God's love is unconditional, constant and unfailing. If we open our hearts, we will receive the Holy Spirit's healing love and forgiveness. God would like to love others through us. We find human fulfillment is not defined by achieving but by becoming more human in our relationship and sharing one another's trials. In loving one another, a wound can be healed.

The song of the heart is the love of God celebrating life with us. This song connects us with others through relationships fostered by the blessings of God's love. When one begins to relate at the heart and soul level, a oneness of which all can be a part is created. Respect and acceptance allow for forgiveness of self and others. A stronger bond of understanding and love will be formed. If we could look into each other's hearts and understand the unique challenges each of us face, we would treat one another much more gently, with more patience, tolerance, care, and LOVE. The conscious act of "being loving" creates a harmonious atmosphere for peaceful relationships.

It brings balance and restores hope to interactions

between people. When the mind is at peace, clear thinking can create harmony. Wouldn't it be glorious if loving attitudes were the standard thought process through which each of us viewed life, just as the Beatle's song says "all you need is love"? What an amazingly simple idea and thought! In a loving world, faith and caring would flow naturally, creating an expectancy in the future-good life can hold. Goodness could flourish as it is passed. It starts with you.

The powerful force of love is:

To matter is to become light
To become light is to be loved
And to love is to truly exist.

Unknown

Love is a part of all lessons learned. Then more texture and depth will permeate the soul, filled with love. True success is coming into your authentic self through Christ's love. The real connection is on the inside of your soul. No person or thing is the answer to our completeness. Love is feeling the fullness and union with God. It fosters the ability to love, serve and forgive others. An abundant life unfolds itself as a steady flow of grace creates love and gratefulness. One's heart then blossoms into a contented, loving heart through acceptance of Jesus' will for each person's life. Through this love, new freedom is born. A spiritual gift is given when one surrenders to God. It's freedom found within you. This freedom becomes a life well lived in being loving.

HOPE

I pray that God will help you overflow with hope in him through the Holy Spirit's power within you.

Romans 15:13

What hope is there in a season of darkness? A deeper faith of amazing grace can grow. It allows us to realize that it isn't so much a matter of hanging on as of being held. A wonderful hope appears for the one who is suffering. Hope looks to what has been real in life—family, friends, and daily grace. God is the true anchor in the rough seas one faces. As the storms of daily life intensify, one needs only to cast the anchor of hope deeper, believing God will guide you.

Adversity may be a burden or a bridge of hope to an unfathomable relationship with God. Since God is good, there can always be hope, even when suffering injustice or hurt. Life may not be easy as not all prayers are answered the way requested. But God gives us hope, making life livable. If one expects only good, what would happen to free will? Would grace and forgiveness play a part in our lives? How would Jesus' extraordinary sacrifice fit? He was the living model of the hope to come! At times one may feel overwhelmed by what is happening. Quiet the mind and listen for the gentle whisper of hope from within. The circumstances can be used to create good in the future.

Of course you'll encounter trouble. But behold a God of power who can take any evil and turn it into a door of hope.

Catherine Marshall

Difficult times, whether they be temporary or illness from which there is no total recovery, can be downright discouraging. Thankfully, we have the hope of knowing the goodness of the Lord. It is not always deliverance from hard circumstances. It is keeping faith and hope alive. They fuel life! When deeper strength is needed, hope on the truths of the Bible and the reality of the Holy Spirit.

No other religion, no other, promises new bodies, hearts and minds. Only in the gospel of Christ do hurting people find such incredible hope.

Joni Eareckson Tada

God helps us realize "all things work together for good to those who love Him." Trials can be misunderstood unless we believe He means all things. Hope infuses life into the most daunting happenings. With hope, one can reach out in that particular moment to thank God for being with you and working out what is best. The brokenness will be restored or rebuilt to form a stronger, more unique you—one who is ignited with hope.

I would have lost heart, unless I had believed that I would see the goodness of the Lord in the land of the living.

Psalms 27:13

As one lets go of hurt and allows constructive thinking to generate healthy, hopeful thought patterns, change begins. Don't allow anyone to take your hope or make you lose your song. In the midst of trouble, rejoice anyway. You can choose what kind of song your heart sings. Let in the habit of hopefulness so it can grow. Hope is confident expectation of blessings to come. Give thanks and praise to God, joyfully, even before the blessings arrive. Through God's grace, things appear in His timing.

A positive thought is the seed of a positive result.

Al-Anon

*I will hope continually and will
praise you yet more and more.*

Psalms 71:14

Jesus, I must trust you, in you I put my hope.

Al-Anon

FAITH

Faith is built in small ways to start. A foundation needs to be laid. The firmness of the foundation must allow for the flexibility required like the sway of the Bay Bridge in San Francisco. The base is an unyielding rock known to weather the assaults that nature throws at it. Like God, the rock, who is unchanging and unmovable—His foundation—allow one to trust and explore with a sense of safety. The sway of life experiences challenges one. By trusting God's guidance, a person will always find a firm foundation beneath one's feet and light permanently shining before you. His present assurance leads through uncertainty to faith.

Trust in the Lord, forever, for the Lord,
the Lord Himself, is the Rock eternal.

Isaiah 26:4

In the Bible, two houses experience the same raging storm. Both structures were identical except for their foundation—one on the sand and the other on 'the' Rock: God. Our lives, like the houses, are similar. We all experience hurt and pain. It's our foundations that differ. When the foundation is founded on God's forgiveness, love and our faith in Jesus Christ, a place of safety is created. A place of comfort and security is carved into the rock of our foundation—God!

Faith is opening one's mind so God's thoughts may flow into our heart and mind. Our faith can move mountains. Listen to God's words as they guide you through life. Human nature and the world changes. In those confusing times, celebrate the unknown. Accept what is, at the present time. This illuminates reality. Then one is ready to listen and see what your next step should be. Let go of struggling and let change begin. Be at peace and give thanks for what is to come. Wait expectantly in faith for gifts each day offers. Have faith; all things will work together for good to those who love God. Trials can be misunderstood unless we believe He means all things. The testing of our faith grows our trust in His faithfulness. Each change creates trust, which develops into hope. Hope infuses life into the most difficult circumstances. With hope comes gratitude, which creates joy in all situations. Joy lightens the heart and gives us the will to live our best life in that particular moment. When one thanks God for being with you and for helping you work out your good in every situation, faith takes root. Opening to blessings available allows one to let go of the past and believe God will pour His love and faith into your heart. This will help release the old feelings and welcome the new. Now one can experience the exhilaration of living life abundantly in FAITH. Even with a world filled with violence, dehumanization, and corruption, one can take a leap of faith.

How do we begin? By reading His words in the Bible and by praying. In reflecting on what one reads, one's dread turns to a healthy respect of trust. We learn He is the only thing that is unchangeable. Give Him the chance to prove He is faithful!

In God's eyes, nothing is impossible. From there, solutions unfold as you relax, staying in tune with God. As you move through each stage, insurmountable problems can be broken down. Like the saying says, "inch by inch it's a cinch." Next, rid yourself of negative attitudes, make necessary decisions, have patience and pray. Through the inquisitive nature planted by God, His children draw on their faith to make exciting breakthroughs. Over the years, planting seed after seed of faith, the belief in the power of God in our life becomes a field of faith, rooted in believing. Add to it the realization one doesn't have to do it alone. This illuminates the truth. God will lighten the load. That's faith! It matters not the size of our faith. What's important is God is at the center. In Matt. 17:20, "faith the size of a mustard seed is enough."

Faith is believing the impossible is possible with His help. Trusting in what cannot be proven, life is an adventure in faith. Faith is not faith if it is seen. True faith is unseen. The eyes of faith make the way clear. Now all things become possible. Faith-filled patience is the key. Patience anchors our soul in hope as we walk in faith.

Although the stress and strain of life
My thread of faith may break,
The cable of His faithfulness
No storm can ever shake.

Al-Anon

At a car wash, your car is propelled on a conveyer belt out of one's control. The dirt is bombarded by cascades of water, soap, and brushes, scrubbing it to a clean and polished shine. Similar to the car, life's storms become a training ground where one gains faith. He cleans you up and sends you on your way to being faithful.

Use now what God has given you,
Count not its worth as small;
God does not ask of you great things,
Just faithfulness—that's all!

Bosch

WISDOM

Prayer needs to be a way of life to gain wisdom. It helps in identification of problems and how to solve them. Praying doesn't take the place of actions. It's a way of gaining the wisdom of how to approach an issue. God becomes a companion who is all-knowing, caring, powerful and is always there to guide us. Pretty Amazing!

Proverbs 3:5-6:

*Trust in the Lord with all your heart
and lean not on your understanding.
In all thy ways acknowledge Him
and He will direct your paths.*

Daily relaxing and making time to meditate helps one grow in wisdom. God renegotiates your pace and path each day. In doing this, joy can be provided on your journey. Quiet moments let us rise above difficulties and tap into the wisdom of the heart. As one prayerfully meditates, your God-given spirit formulates thoughts into awaiting answers enriching each new day. One can become confused by evil disguised as a minister of good. To avoid deception and temptation, be sure to learn God's truths, so you are not led astray by false words and people. In the Faust drama, it is said, "People do not know the devil is there even when he has them by the throat."

A plumb line is used to help create correct measurements in buildings. God's plumb line is His words through His commandments and the Bible. Your obedience to His words makes straight how to live life. The door is open when reading with a hearing heart. His wisdom radiates a guiding light, taking you from helplessness to joy, peace and knowledge. Wise decisions come from receiving the gift of insight to any challenge. Sometimes, the answers arrive gently, others in pain.

God whispers to us in our pleasures, speaks in our conscience, but shouts in our pain.

C.S. Lewis, The Problem of Pain (Collins, 1973)

The light of God can illuminate the mind with wisdom. His love can open and enlarge the heart, creating an attitude of patience, compassion, and kindness. These gifts stimulate behaviors more caring and wise. It gets us through troubles and helps calm any anxiety. Wisdom then flows serenity from within lighting the way to the best outcome. Your inner compass directs the heart to find needed answers.

Bits of the light filtered through the windows
of heaven illuminate the wisdom in our hearts.
Heaven is God's heart. Let nothing dim the
mind the light that shines from within.

Maya Angelou

Any problem turns into a lesson from which wisdom grows. Upon listening, the silent heart responds with God's infallible guidance. Gently nudging one to what is right for you. God's wisdom is your legacy of blessings. Temptations and defeat will not triumph with him in your corner. What emanates from the sacred center within is the divine nature of your character. It is walking with integrity. In Hebrew, it means, "to walk with sincerity," not to be faultless. Faultlessness is God's domain, not ours. To seek the Lord's mercy and wisdom is ours. One is not expected to be perfect but to listen to God's words and walk with integrity.

WORRY

When worries surface, acknowledge them. Talk to God and ask for His grace to help you overcome any fears. Now allow yourself to write them down and then share them with a trusted friend. You may not always like what you hear from both your friend and God but listen. In time "he shall strengthen your heart." Psalm 27:14.

Is it a problem or an inconvenience? Life is chockfull of inconvenience. One's idea of a problem and inconvenience is blurred. Trivial issues burst to monumental dimension as we use our "Quick Shop" mentality such as a car repair versus no transportation. We think today one is entitled to perfection and the sooner, the better. Tempers flare over what are just plain minor problems. When one calms the mind, most worries decrease to minor bothers. One can find fear, worry and stress balloon life situations into anxiety-laden thoughts that may or may not occur. They usually don't. These thoughts steal one's joy from the day ahead. Unproductive hours are spent on events one can neither change nor control. The realization that there is a gracious power ultimately in control can bring peace to the soul. Rejoice and listen.

Real optimism is aware of problems but recognizes solutions, knows difficulties but believes they can be overcome, has reason to complain but chooses to smile.

William Arthur Ward

Since worries usually never materialize, resolve to expect the best from circumstances and people. This inspires the unfolding of positive outcomes. It's contagious! Positive energy illuminates the way to good results. Worry wastes precious time and energy. It doesn't change the outcome. It only ruins the present moments. One can get weighted down in the minutia of life. So grab hold of thoughts and write them down. Answers will take shape, allowing one to become more centered. Search now for God's wisdom to guide you in a positive direction. Aware of divine guidance in decision-making, one finds the way around obstacles. He helps you to look to the future with confidence. Now worry about nothing. Pray about everything.

1 Peter 5:7 TLB

Let (God) have all your worries and cares,
for He is always thinking about you and
watching everything that concerns you.

SUFFERING

God planted the gift of free will as part of human nature. He did not create mindless robots. The misuse of free will has ended in a problem-ridden society. It spills over to all human beings. When we find it hard to understand why something has taken place, we are not able to always see the complications caused by our world. They run deep and are varied. Our task is to seek God. If we listen to His wisdom, we will emerge wiser. The scarring we experience tells the tale of survival, healing, and growth. Each of us has a story to tell. All are walking wounded who can either hide the pain or find a way to speak about our wounds in such a way others can be helped by our story. Your resilient spirit and wisdom acquired from God can be a healing balm to hurting souls and to you.

Suffering tends to be caused by invading germs, human evil, and poor decisions. These issues draw us, humans, to be fully human, filled with truer sensitivity to one another's plight. Hopefully, it increases our awareness of both our needs and others. In the midst of it, there is an ongoing fight to find God. The spiritual struggle is to see God's face both in the good and bad times. Knowing He outlasts all times.

Our world works in concert with our choices and outside forces. A car out of control on ice doesn't miss the natural consequences of an accident just because you are a Christian. As a result of free will, the natural results occur. God doesn't create tragic circumstances. Our world is at the center.

No one is exempt from life's difficulties. There are seasons of growth in those times, which are hard to accept. The acceptance and overcoming of these trials indeed strengthen one in mind and spirit. Emotional muscle is built. A desire for a "candy-like" God creates feelings of bitterness. When things don't go as one wants or plans, anger can appear. The ability to accept and be at peace no matter the outcome helps one to live well. It is not always the easiest but definitely the best way.

Restrictions of body or environment need not limit one. Embrace it as a growing place. Limits help one mature, strengthen us and help one to become the person you wish to become. By accepting God's guidance, no matter how hopeless things seem, He will create awareness of how best to live through every circumstance. The presence of God can create strength of heart and peace of mind. The misconception is that if one is truly faithful, one will be delivered from adversity. The promise is He will deliver one "in" adversity. The very strain of life builds spiritual strength. Without any strain, no growth happens. Unexercised muscles weaken, so life left untested by trouble becomes complacent and lax. During difficult times, God provides moment-by-moment grace to help you.

We also rejoice in our suffering, because we know that suffering, produces perseverance; perseverance, character and hope. And does not disappoint us because God has poured out His love into our hearts by the Holy Spirit, whom He has given us.

Romans 5: 3-5

Suffering perhaps becomes the yeast that makes one rise above life's troubles. Upon taking a step back from what is going on, there is a realization: pain and suffering are born out of an impure world. Don't expect it to make sense. One's limited understanding questions why. Only God can mold these trials into something glorious in Christ's time.

For all the heartaches and the tears,
For gloomy days and fruitless years
I do give thanks, for now I know
These were the things that helped me grow!

L.E. Thayer

FORGIVENESS

God knows the deep places our lives go through. He lifts our hearts when distressed and gives hope through His mercy. His loving kindness is available for the asking. It might not be what is asked for but what is best. A time will come down the line where the truth will no longer be hidden if one is willing to be quiet and listen to your heart. Until then, He continues to love all equally and provides the opportunity for salvation. No matter what has happened, God is merciful and will forgive if asked. Nothing you have not done or done will cause one to be unworthy of God's love and forgiveness.

One's differences or disagreements are not worth giving up the peace within the soul. Releasing all feelings of being slighted, having to be right or needing your way allows forgiveness to cultivate tranquility within. Thus anger dealt with quickly and without meaning to do harm can have a positive effect on your countenance. Forgiveness of our self or another is a uniquely healing gift each of us can provide. The holding on and in of resentment and animosity causes one to extend the pain. It's a double whammy. First, one is hurt by someone then by hanging on to the hurt it reinjures you over and over. In forgiving and not accepting what was said or done as right, you are allowing forgiveness to help you let go and to heal. By releasing negative feelings, your heart and mind fill with God's love. Another's love will never satisfy for it's filled with human frailties. Only God's love can paralyze hatred.

The need to be forgiving and to forgive will reappear through our life. Without forgiveness, anger and hatred take root. Only love can release the stony heart.

To forgive is not easy yet necessary. Grace, not retaliation, starts the process. Choosing, over and over, to let go of resentment, one finally comes to terms with the knowledge it is the most healing way. One no longer becomes consumed with anger. Now, fully ready to focus on living each new day, a chance becomes available to avoid being resentful.

*We can let the circumstances of our lives harden
us so that we become increasingly resentful
and afraid, or we can let them soften us,
make us kinder. You always have the choice.*

Dalai Lama

Forgiveness is an act of will, not emotion. God will provide the feeling if we provide the desire. Don't let others be stealers of your peace. Know they were wrong but don't let it steal your peace. It takes a period of time to allow thoughts of forgiveness to begin to work in you. Gradually, God will help you release the hurt, changing pain to feelings of peace and healing. One is not able to hold bitterness and God's grace at the same time.

Forgiveness is not an occasional act. It is a constant action.

Martin Luther King, Jr.

Steps to Help One Forgive:

1. Cherish the forgiveness you receive from God.
2. Turn the person completely over to God. Be sure to leave them in God's hands.
3. Release bitterness.
4. Repeat as needed.

Until you forgive, the power is in the unforgiveness and the unforgiven!

RELATIONSHIPS

A successful, loving relationship is more than finding the right partner. It is being the right partner. Our desire to always be right has no place in a relationship. Communication, respect (equality through Christ), unwavering perseverance and prayer are key to creating a lasting relationship with our mate. All this in partnership with God. The need to control, criticize and become combative results in an atmosphere constantly filled with frustration and irritation. A life of malcontent results.

Insignificant quarrels waste emotional and physical energy. The ability to tame negative energy allows one to see what one's mate is thinking and feeling. It can bring wisdom and healing. The lesson learned will reappear until we recognize and learn it.

Unacceptable behavior can be given acceptable names to hide the truth. Exaggeration in truth is lying. Nerves are just plain an out of control temper. The desire to overcome a negative habit is to honestly name it and repent.

*The tongue is a little member
and boosts great things*

James 3:5

'Can't' and 'won't' are words with immense power. If we say, "we can't do something," like understand our mate or child—it blocks any sincere effort. In choosing to say, "with the help of God, I will try," a new openness allows hope and a change in attitude. The essence of the situation is altered. Walls can start to crumble, feelings soften and hope rises, setting the stage for healing. Forgiveness is now fostered.

Our deepest longing is to be loved by another. When one doesn't feel safe, a closing off or down starts. It becomes hard to trust and let someone into your heart. Numbness sets in, affecting the heart's soul. One needs to surrender the hurts by trusting God to guide our steps. Step by step, the hearing of the still, quiet voice of God in our heart slowly releases the barriers, and it becomes easier and easier to be more loving, forgiving and giving in a relationship. It all takes time. The other person may not ever heal, yet, you will. In certain situations, you may have to move on from that relationship. Thankfully, you can heal with God's help.

Our relationships with another can be like a broken fence needing mending. You need to get the proper tools and supplies together. God can supply the tools required to mend a marriage if both are willing. Through faith and hard work, a worn out broken down relationship can be mended, creating a stronger three-tiered cord—God, you and your mate.

All have unhealed places within. We need each other,

yet we seem to needle one another. Thus the heart may need repairs. Repairs create a shift in thought patterns. Upon making the shift, God can then work at teaching us how to forgive and heal what has been broken. Through forgiving, a real honest relationship can be cobbled together if both parties wish for a healthy relationship to form. Sometimes one needs to start the process before the other becomes willing to participate. It can be a slow progression. One can easily lose sight of hopes and dreams shared as a couple. Everyday life gets in the way. One can begin to dwell on the past mistakes and disappointments your mate has made. They become a source of irritation. God can show the way to stop looking at the past and look for the good. He helps release negative thoughts and helps one look to the future, if asked. It will likely be an ongoing praying for what is necessary, day by day. Focusing on flaws and failures whether they be yours or someone else's, keeps one stagnant. The forgiving love of Jesus allows growth and the rediscovery of the good in one's self and others. All wish for a "relationship made in heaven." The truth is it has to be worked out here on Earth.

The way to start:

1. Let go of anger by asking God's help, over and over.
2. Desire to forgive and to begin.
3. Look for the good.
4. Release hurt to God.
5. Spend quality time together.
6. Acknowledge the needs of the other.
7. Express loving kindness.
8. Repeat as necessary.

Forgive, but you don't have to accept unacceptable behavior or trust. If positive changes are taking place, make sure you begin to make positive changes. If you both don't make forward changes, then allow yourself to forgive so you can let go and move on with your life.

The willingness to focus on what you agree on and respecting another's right to a different opinion opens communication. Accepting and accentuating the positive qualities of one who differs creates a bond on which to build a harmonious start. A start seeking the goodness in another and loving one as one is. A human can choose his or her actions. Your choice of being willing or willful is up to you. The will to think the best of someone can bring the best out. With faith-filled prayers, a relationship's transformation is possible, prayer-by-prayer in most situations. It is worth a try for sure. The road may be rocky, but with the tools of forgiveness, hope, love and both partners willing, a way can be chiseled a piece at a time. The truth applied with love allows the heart gently to hear the spirit of God as it mends the relationship.

It takes the time and effort of both people to make the necessary changes,

The tongue of the wise brings healing.

Proverbs 12:18

True life is lived when tiny changes occur.

Leo Tolstoy

Each positive change alters one's outlook. It's never too late to make changes to who you are at this present time.

INNER PEACE

Inner peace brings quiet to the soul. It transcends the outer challenges. Irritations become minor, and worries are transformed by God's peace. Peace becomes constant and eternal. While outside events are fleeting, you begin the process of finding your authentic self. You search inside your soul for answers. No one or thing is the answer to completeness. Abundant life unfolds through grace. It teaches appreciation and gratefulness. The contented heart is found in acceptance of Jesus' will for your life.

Through this process, a new freedom is born. This freedom is the spiritual gift given when surrendering to God. A freedom found in being loving. One of the keys to inner peace is forgiveness. Not allowing yourself to take offense brings personal growth and the peace you seek. Next, try to understand the reason for what is said or done. This can create empathy. You may even find yourself caring about the harm he or she is doing to themselves. Healing for both of you could come from your prayers for understanding. The spirit of peace moves life forward. Resistance slows what can take place. The gentle flow of circumstances on their natural course may require finding a way over or around obstacles. Difficult situations do occur but learning to flow along not resist is the best plan. Butting against problems is tiring. It's a choice to ask for wisdom and wait for an answer or resist. Spiritual guidance can transform your days ahead. Change comes upon acceptance of God's will and help. This spiritual change will carry you through what is to come. Changes will come—embrace them—don't fear change. Possibilities open up that can define who you will become. These changes can make others uncomfortable. Allow yourself to trust God's grace not your will. God is your strength. He doesn't want you to suffer. He wants wholeness for each of us. Let go of fear and worry. God promises His love no matter what.

Marcus Aurelius said,

Man must be arched and buttressed from within, else the temple wavers to the dust.

Staying close to Jesus allows you limitless emotional and physical healing. His presence in quiet times strengthens your faith and fills you with peace. If you let your emotions rule, tensions rise. When all parts of the body function in a more relaxed state, focusing on His presence, the brain works at peak performance. A tempo in which positive changes occur, benefiting your whole being.

PURPOSE

Work is success oriented. A purpose filled vocation is faith filled with greater meaning—it is life-giving. Upon hearing vocation or calling, the mind might shut down. It's too churchy, uncool or out of the realm of possibility. One can see the real difference between a job and a vocation is finally allowing God to help you see what is meaningful work, which lifts up others in some way. Today more and more people's jobs have become their God. Work creeps into homes via cell phones, iPods and computers. Work becomes one's source of fulfillment. He or she loses perspective and balance by placing God and family in last place. They receive what is left over of our energy creating frustration and many times misplaced anger. Until one realizes the gaining of more and more things never satisfy, one's life can become the burial ground of insignificance. Life may feel futile. The truth is if one believes in God, life has a purpose since He is in control. An ordinary being who believes in an extraordinary God will find purpose.

*We have received the Spirit that is
from God, so that we may understand
the gift bestowed on us by God.*

1 Corinthians 2:12

A sense of abundant wholeness flows from a true purpose-filled life. It allows the enriching aspects of life to reach their full potential. All limitations are released. The freedom of the Holy Spirit rises to clear the pathway so one may find purpose. What is beginning to be imagined can become a reality, satisfying to the soul. The dreams of living your best life are fostered. A nobler purpose appears to you.

As Mother Teresa said,

In this life, we cannot do great things. We can only do small things with great love.

Each action no matter its size impacts the world. Better it to be of a higher purpose. The act of loving and doing for one another brings about remarkable changes. From giving and receiving our heart finds fulfillment, purpose, and joy. As one lives a life of gratitude, one is no longer preoccupied with self. Instead in serving humanity, this loving is the essence and purpose of life.

'For I know the plans I have for you,' declares the Lord. 'Plans to prosper you and not to harm you, plans to give you hope and a future — seek Me with all your heart.'

Jeremiah 29:11

GRATITUDE

Each morning one rises either with gratitude or grumbling. Simple everyday activities are miracles, gifts most precious to behold to those with limited abilities. It's easy to take for granted the five senses and their functions. When no challenge occurs, entitlement becomes the norm. The simplest things of life resonate with pleasure: cool soft pillows, fresh sheets, a gentle breeze—each to be ignored or savored. It's a choice. Consider now how you view life. Is it a boring routine or a gratifying blessing? It is up to you to choose what you think and do.

Reflect upon your present blessings - of which every man has many—not on your past misfortunes, of which all men have some.

Charles Dickens

Life altering events, some of which make one want to say no not I or why me, come to each one of us. Raging with anger changes nothing, brings no peace and stagnates possibilities. All feel anger at first but continuing to live your anger, over and over, achieves nothing. Blessings can be found if one is willing to push aside self-pity and appreciate the simple blessings one takes for granted. Simple pleasures are the most satisfying. All else is chasing the wind, leaving you empty grasping for more.

I have learned it is the sweet, simple things of life, which are the real ones after all.

Laura Ingalls Wilder

There are options in life, fear and anger or gratitude, and love. Gratitude permits one to see things differently. Christ will take the hurt and pain, then work it toward a better outcome. Neither of these responses will change the circumstances one Iota. The attitude only changes the way one deals with the situation. The metamorphosis, which takes place through thoughts of gratitude, arrives in believing another life of far more significance waits in the wings.

The hardships endured become faded memories. A season of amazing growth begins. When looking now with the eyes of gratitude beauty and substance is added to each day. An appreciation of sights and sounds fill the brain. Your attention turns to the good in life. There comes a blossoming and hopeful feeling within, spilling over to others. It's catching.

JOY

Each of us by our very nature can find much to fill us with JOY. Our five senses, nature and all the wonders the world possesses can create a joyful spirit. Joy is the internal gladness our heart releases into one's life. When one praises and gives thanks, your relationship with God allows His blessings to unfold. Your thankfulness is the language, which brings joy to your heart. A joyful continence encourages all kinds of healing, relieves anxiety, helps to reset priorities and clears the thought process. Now you can see the blessings otherwise one might overlook. Simple moments of nature, a loved one's phone call can now bring comfort. This joy can lift the spirit inviting divine joy to fill the heart and mind. It energizes positiveness, infusing life into what one says and does. Joy rises to the surface. The fullness of joy is grounded in Jesus Christ who is the same today, yesterday and always. Pleasure is fleeting depending on one's circumstances. Joy is inward not changed by outside stimuli. Joy is found in giving from the fullness of your heart what one can give. Joy is the zest God gives to life. A zest for living is also found in believing the best is yet to unfold. The resonating joy from within the soul adds quality to everyday occurrences. It brings new life to living and helps life to be experienced in all its fullness. Our attitude, not circumstances, is the true foundation of joy. This new appreciation acknowledges the presence of God's grace to live fully no matter the circumstance. Real joy comes from deep within one's soul.

CONCLUSION

Jesus through His choice of common fishermen to be His disciples made it plain; ordinary people are called by God to do His work. The birthplace of Jesus, His parents, His followers, and friends were all people like you and me.

He was honored and feared by church leaders, kings, queens and government officials. They all were His witnesses in one way or another. Being a spectator in life's arena makes life risky. One begins to find life discouraging; God's words lose their worth. When you choose to venture out in faith, it may seem to be questionable. The far greater risk is being a spectator. We are all called to get in the game.

Be the change you want to see in the world.

Gandhi

In our weakness, one gains strength through Jesus. His indwelling grows as one relinquishes control. This allows the Grace of God to free you. The Spirit, not the law releases one. The Spirit infuses faith, hope, trust and the love of God into our heart and mind. Then the mind can be renewed and transformed. One's being can transform into a restful trust in Almighty God. Through this renewal, one becomes justified by Grace. Salvation is yours for the asking. What will follow is God's promise, the Holy Spirit will start to work all things out for you in the end.

Salvation comes by the Grace of God. There is still confusion about "good works." Good works aren't necessary to please God, as some are not physically or mentally able. The goodness of the Holy Spirit can supply what is needed. A flowering tree may begin to live within each person's heart, Jesus will come to live there and be the gardener if you desire it. Just ask. He will make it grow inside and help weed it when necessary. The weeds of sin begin to fade and beautiful flowers of love and kindness take their place. One continually needs to pull out the sin weeds by asking Jesus for His help and forgiveness. The flowers blossom into a bouquet of loveliness.

I am here, Lord, rooted in earth and mire.
You are heavenly, celestial and holy.
Where do we meet, Lord?
Who knows the way?
Don't fear; only believe and pray.

MAO

What an excellent ground of hope and confidence we have when we reflect upon these three things in prayer—The Father's love, The Son's merit and the Spirit's power!

Thomas Manton

*Always there—watching, waiting,
hoping you will call out.*

*See you—stumbling, falling, doing
what you think is best.*

*Numb to the truth God is always
willing to let you rest.*

MAO

Jesus is all the world to me,
My life, my joy, my all;
He is my strength from day to day
Without Him, I would fall.

Thompson

How are we to be sure this is all true? God's word in the Bible says, "If you declare with your mouth, 'Jesus is Lord,' and believe in your heart that God raised Him from the dead. You will be saved."

Some people require scholarly proof based on facts as did investigative journalist, Lee Strobel. He traveled far and wide to discredit Christ's life, death and resurrection. Instead, he found vast amounts of documentation to its truth.

Be joyful in hope, patient in affliction, faithful in prayer.

Romans 12:12

May all families become enriched.
My hope is you may glean insights
To help you grow in faith as you journey
Through your life.

The wish I make
The prayer I pray
May my life touch
Others on the way.

MAO

*Knowledge of the secret of the kingdom
of heaven has been given to you*

Matt. 13:11

www.ingramcontent.com/pod-product-compliance
Lightning Source LLC
Chambersburg PA
CBHW060529030426
42337CB00021B/4194